T0196908

# Rear View Reflections

SAVOI RAGS

**BALBOA**.
PRESS
A DIVISION OF HAY HOUSE

Balboa Press books may be ordered through booksellers or by contacting:

Balboa Press
A Division of Hay House
1663 Liberty Drive
Bloomington, IN 47403
www.balboapress.com
1 (877) 407-4847

Print information available on the last page.

ISBN: 978-1-5043-8426-1 (sc)
ISBN: 978-1-5043-8427-8 (e)

Library of Congress Control Number: 2017910846

Balboa Press rev. date: 09/05/2017

# Contents

# Face-to-Face

The hardest thing I have ever done is
come face-to-face with myself,
Holding myself accountable for
what I say I am going to do.
Maturity is doing what you know to do,
But why do I do the total opposite?
When I look deep into my eyes, I
see a perfect, invisible me,
The wisest one I know staring back at me.
Tapping into my greatness is what she is all about.
I could fool the world but never myself
Face-to-face.

# My Honey!

My honeypot is the sweetest love
I have ever experienced.
He always enjoys my company and is loyal as hell.
He is playful, my wild man,
And intuitive—he knows when I need
much more of his oh-so-real love.
Many times I don't even know he's around.
He's so laid back, he's mellow,
and he just loves to chill.
He snores like an obese man, believe it or not.
He's my Honeypot, my Tater Tot, my Babe!
My eleven-year-old Lhasa Apso.

# Who Ya Gonn' Be?

It's so easy for any of us to flow
with smooth sailing.
The big question is who ya gonn' be
when going through the storms?
Deliver me from those who have an
opinion about how you should
Handle the issues of life.
Whose life is this?
Enjoy the smooth sailing because all of
us have the opportunity to discover
Who ya gonn' be!
Character-building experiences reveal
Who ya gonn' be!

# Paradise

Just the thought of embracing you
Puts the widest smile on my face.
Know that just hearing your
voice makes me open up
More and more, like a flower budding.
You tell me it's so sweet.
Finally, I'm home to the lover I always
felt was made for only me.
Welcome to paradise, baby.

# Grown, Huh?

I vividly remember how I could
hardly wait to be eighteen,
Couldn't wait to be grown—
or was eighteen grown?
Sure, I could drink if I wanted to, go
to clubs, and officially decide
To do it, if I wanted to.
At that age, should I really have been
making some of those life-
Defining decisions?
Couldn't wait to be grown—or was I?
In reality, I was legal but definitely not grown.
Being really grown is determined by the person.
Couldn't wait to be grown, huh?

# True Wealth

What a friend you have been,
Always there for me
Through thick and thin.
You have been on assignment—each
part never dodging its responsibility,
Adjusting even when I had no idea
of the need for adjustment,
And beautiful in every aspect:
sight, touch, and taste.
Even I say to Him, "Wow, thank
you for blessing me
From head to teeth to toe."
So don't hate because I take care of myself.
To many I look the same as in
high school—why or how?
My first wealth is my health.

# Never in Vain

I've got one life to live.
I live it to the fullest.
Different decisions I have made.
Different choices I have chosen.
Each thing I have
Loved through,
Hurt through,
And journeyed through
Has helped me be who I am today.
I have never been one for regrets,
And I am not about to start now!
I am thankful for all the life lessons
I have learned and can share,
can inspire others with,
Because my journey in this life is *never* in vain.

# My First Big Heartbreak

I remember always wondering
whom I would marry.
Then we met.
For the first time in my life, I felt
someone really got me.
We were wonderful friends who
intellectually jived.
Later, becoming sweethearts
Was a natural segueway.
Our kisses I still remember,
And the park was our favorite seclusion.
Talk of marriage and when was
the right time for us
Was so exciting
Until that Christmas I was to meet your parents,
Only to find out I just wasn't good
enough for you or your family.
I guess it's true:
You do marry the family.

# Best Friends

Early on, we were two peas in a pod.
Fun! Fun! Fun!
Our brothers were boys, so we naturally hung out.
Then we realized we had a lot
of things in common.
Remaining virgins as long as we
could was one of them.
Remember what we would say
of the ones doing it?
"Yeah, they are so fast," as we
called it in the South,
Proud that we were not.
It was nice to reconnect a while back.
My biggest disappointment?
We never really got to know each other again.
Our conversations hid behind forwarded
e-mails instead of real talk.
I miss what we once had!

# My Buddy

Never ever *ever* do You lead me wrong.
My life just flows when I acknowledge You first.
I call You my secret sauce.
Thank You for always being there.
My life is so sweet just because of You,
My navigational system leading,
guiding, and directing me.
I know I am never alone.
Because of You, I literally live in the zone.
My buddy, God, the divine,
infinite, intelligent source.

# Savor Every Moment

I finally have learned how to take
time and smell the roses,
Savor every moment.
When I do, I don't just exist—
I live!
Minute by minute,
Second by second,
Hour by hour,
Day by day,
Week by week,
Month by month,
And year by year.
I then never wonder,
Where did the time go?
Where did the year go?
I know, because I was there.
Every single second
I was truly present!

# My Lemonade

I just never liked the taste,
So I didn't drink or hardly drank it.
Then in college I gained fifteen pounds.
Frantically, I called my dad,
And he told me that I never drink enough of it—
Water.
He said, "Did you know that if you
were in a desert three days, you
Would survive if you had water alone?"
No! But I thought, *You've got to be kidding me.*
So I forced myself to stop every hour
from studying and drink it.
It's now my elixir of life,
With a bowl of lemons, that is—no added sugar.
My lemonade.

# Brilliant

You never know who will really live
up to or exceed their potential.
Oh sure, we all have an idea of who.
Truth is, only you know the flame
that burns inside of you.
Only you know the dreams you play
over and over in your head.
Only you design the life you want.
Brilliant—
That's what you are,
Living by your own lights,
Soaring like an eagle,
Redefining greatness,
Making me so proud of all your
endeavors and accomplishments!
Thanks for truly stepping up.
You inspire me, as I am sure you do others.

# Momzi

I was a shy little girl,
But people don't believe me.
To an extent, I still really am shy.
But my entry into this world through you
Totally redirected my path.
"Sweetie, would you like to learn
how to play the piano?"
"Yes, Mommy," I would reply.
"Would you like to learn how to sew?"
"Yes, Mommy!"
Before I even knew it, I began to
blossom right before my own eyes.
I used to hate practicing public speaking for 4-H.
Now, speaking is one of my greatest assets.
Thanks for nurturing me to come out of
my shell into the person I continue
To grow into now.
Thanks for taking your assessment
of me so seriously.
Years later, I renamed you affectionately Momzi.
Momzi, I honor you!

# Cutie Patootie

An adorable little puppy,
I am so frightened and confused—
after a long plane ride,
I find two perfect strangers waiting for me.
I am relieved to be on the ground,
But don't understand all the noises or commotion.
I miss my momma and my sisters.
This is my first time away from
them, and I'm in a box I hate.
Not sure if I did something wrong or just … what?
Where are they?
A big man holds me, and a nice
lady is talking to me.
I have no idea what she is saying,
But I feel that I am theirs and they are mine.
Lickey, lickey is what I do over and over again,
My way of showing affection.
I am named after the late singer Prince.
My new mom nicknamed me her Cutie Patootie.

# On Purpose

I love this time of year,
When I reflect on my highs and
lows of the previous year
And reach forward to better my best.
I hold myself accountable to
soar like never before,
Turn all lemons to lemonade,
And see the good, the best, of every situation.
Now, time to design my life for 2011.
I am so excited about my new
refreshed vision for my life:
I will enjoy it to the fullest
On my terms,
By my lights,
On purpose!

# ManZu

One minute you are my wild man.
The next minute you are snoring
like there is no tomorrow,
Totally content with just being.
I touch you and feel
Soothed,
Refreshed,
Grounded.
You've taught me true unadulterated love,
Excitement from just the little things,
Understanding, and your snort of affirmation.
You're never a bother nor a fuss,
My confidant; you are all ears.
My workout partner.
You've given me my very best years, ManZu!

# Down-Home Cookin'

For years I've said that I can't cook.
Most recently, my friend reminded me
Oh yes, I can!
Over the years I've allowed my
flame to be put out.
My flame was rekindled recently!
I love cooking, enjoying an awesome meal.
Even sweeter is when guests join us too.
Looking forward to continuing
to explore in this arena,
I have much more appreciation
for home-cooked meals.
There's nothing like it—
Healthy, Southern-style,
Down-home cookin'.

# Release, Refocus, Renew

The shackles have been broken.
No more tug-of-war.
Relax and enjoy your life to the fullest
While I do the same.
Thank you for all the
Inspiration to write and
Express myself more and more.
Thanks for showing me that if I
can think it, I can ink it.
Thanks for being
A mirror reflecting back to me
What I admire in you, I am and try to walk in too.
I've been too close to the forest to see the trees,
But now I'm released, refocused, renewed.

# Who Are You, Really?

What do you call it when you
love someone and still
Realize that you really don't
even know him or her?
Who are you, really?
What makes you tick?
What's your favorite color?
How do you spend your downtime?
What kind of honey are you?
Reveal yourself to me.
What kind of friend are you?
I want to get to know you—
Not the person I *thought* I knew.
One layer at a time, I'd like to get to know
Who you are, really.

# Just Be

True to my own lights,
Doing my absolute best,
Giving God all the glory,
Inspired to tap into my greatness more and more,
To understand, feel, and communicate
the true essence of me,
I thank God for the barometer I
now have to gauge love
The way I deserve to be loved.
Never allowing anything again to be a hindrance,
deterrent, or stumbling block,
I now view them as motivators,
inspirations, and regulators
Reminding me of all I want, desire,
and deserve in my life:
My fire, my light, my safety net,
My most powerful and positive energy–
Where I can just be!

# Literally Let Go!

I no longer hold onto your heart or pull on it
By my thoughts, words, or vibes.
I am a blessing in your life.
I breathe life into you.
I encourage, inspire, and support
you exactly where you are.
I celebrate your successes and
encourage you to continue
To strive to be your absolute best.
Still—I release you, babe!
Literally, I let go.

# Poetry in Motion

Dancing is still my absolutely fave thing to do!
I just lose myself.
The great melodies, bass, and awesome grooves
Pull me in so seductively.
I just let my body express what I
hear and how it makes me feel.
Poetry in motion is what dancing is for me—
So much so that I will even wrap my knees
If I want to dance the night away!
Old school is my favorite because of all the fond
Memories it brings.
Jazz and classical come straight behind.
Would you like to
Dance the night away?

# Struttin' My Stuff

Music, cameras, and fashions light up the runway.
While struttin' my stuff, I'm in
character for my apparel.
I always thought I'd be a professional.
Here is my Hollywood.
Nontraditional is my beauty, I'm told.
I lose myself, as though I am on the dance floor.
I always thought I would be a
fashion designer as well.
Who knows? You never know.
What I know for sure is that I
blossom in this environment.
It is my wheelhouse and so much of who I am.
I am a creative being.
I don't try to dress differently. I am just me—
Sincerely, fiercely, and authentically
*me.*

# Designer in the Midst

It's never too late to pursue my dreams.
No matter how I look at it, it's
been a dream for years
To be a designer.
It all started with learning to sew at six years old.
Sewing for me was not only a wonderful
release, but I loved creating.
I literally could not stop once I started.
I would compete in 4-H, and because
I was sewing *Vogue* patterns
At such an early age, they thought I
didn't make many of my garments.
Over the years, I haven't sewn as
much, but I create and coordinate
Regularly within my wardrobe.
Some express themselves through words,
But I express myself creatively in
art—the wearable kind.

# Solitude

Everything seems amplified:
The sound of the second hand on the clock,
And the sound of air or heat going on and off.
Other than all the thoughts
running through my mind,
I can hear a pin drop.
Shh!
I just landed in the sphere of the ultimate!
Solitude.

# Feel

Feel! It guides me in every area of my life.
I call it my gut.
When it's not right, it feels like
butterflies in my stomach.
When I am on the right path, I just
have an awesome peace.
Much of my life has been led by
this powerful aspect,
Whether I knew, understood, or
even thought it or not.
For me, I acknowledge Him,
And He directs my path
Directed by how it *feels*!

# Confidence Comes in Doing

So you wonder how I can be so sure of myself.
You can be guaranteed that I have
not always felt this way.
I, like you, have done things that
I just was not good at.
Just like a baby making his or her first step,
Confidence comes in doing.
So over the years I performed
past my understanding
And many times past my ability,
Only to learn more and more about myself,
To gradually feel better and better
About my new challenge.
Not just in thinking or in talking but in the
Doing, confidence comes.

# I Win

The game of life continues to reveal to me
Its similarity to a real sports game.
One is always trying to win:
Faith vs. fear.
To learn that fear is contaminated faith
Is scary enough. Unbelief is
synonymous with fear.
This reminds me of my daily
quest to reside in *faith*,
Making sure my actions line up
with my belief: *faith*.
So even if I go back and forth,
In the end, I *win*. I have *faith*,
That is!

# Alignment

It's all got to jive—
My thoughts, words, and feelings.
Like a good old school song,
Harmonizing like no other,
Agreement is what it also is—
Not divided in any aspect.
Nothing can divide my attention.
While it may look like I've got it all together,
I do not. I continue to adjust,
Just as the jet continues to adjust midair.
I'm insuring my path is smooth, calm, and as one
So my *thoughts*, *words*, and *feelings*
Agree, which is alignment—
Deliberate creation.

# Just Say Nothing

It's easier said than done
To not say anything.
I'm reminded that anyone who
understands spiritual
Laws understands the maxim
"Watch what you say!"
Never ever do I want to have to
Eat my words;
Nor do I want to put poison out on anyone,
So it is true—
Death and life are in the power of the tongue.
I choose life!
If I cannot find something
Positive or affirming to say,
I just say *nothing* at all!

# Not a Dress Rehearsal

To be absent from the body is to
be present with the Lord.
I still wonder about loved ones or
friends I knew personally—
What did they experience as they went
from mortality to immortality?
Some who came close to it say
they saw a bright light
Yet were blessed to remain in
the land of the living.
What thoughts are they experiencing?
How did their lives flash to them?
What really mattered in the end?
Live life to the fullest.
This is *so* not a dress rehearsal!

# Your People

As I journey through this wonderful life,
I receive gifts, many gifts, along the way
From those who are not only on the same page
But also in the same book!
How profound!
Many times without any contact
for months or even years,
We just pick up where we
Left off as though it was just yesterday, leaving me
Feeling more connected than I do many times
With my own family.
What a blessing to get this gift
wrapped in human flesh.
Who are *your* people?

# Undeniable Peace

I know—to most I should be a basket case
After hitting rock bottom in several
areas all at the same time,
But I am the most sane, most relaxed,
Most at peace I have ever been in the storm,
Having recently truly connected
with the real *me*, my core,
The greater one within me.
I am seeing assets about me that
I never ever knew I had.
I love growing through this.
Instead of hating this part of my destination
As I used to in the past,
I know, I call it that good old
Unexplainable, undeniable *peace*.

# Judge Not

I am no different from the next—
Hating to be judged, yet judging.
"What's that, you hypocrite?"
I can always change the subject or
Find something nice to say—my choice.
I choose to no longer allow
Myself to get reeled in
As I have allowed myself to do lately.
When reminded, I say to myself,
"Stop!" or "No poison!"
I need to get that big pole out of
my own eye first, okay?
I am choosing to *focus* on the
divinity within each of us,
Choosing to *vibrate* the highest! To soar!

# Trust

To truly trust is true surrender,
True release.
Trust makes us vulnerable at first—we risk it all
Only to find that life is a total risk.
If you really think about it,
What do you do?
Stay in the bleachers where
It is supposedly safe,
Or come out on the field and play? Live. Risk.
With a century behind my belt,
I now know how to trust myself better,
Relying on my instincts and hunches,
Whether I understand them or not.
To truly *trust* is to genuinely live.

# By My Own Lights

I love who I am.
I love the person I choose to be.
I conscientiously make my choices in life.
I know that I strive to be prudent,
To have wise thoughts before I act.
I'm just doing my best with doing that.
What I am excited about right now in my life is
The new lease I have given myself
To no longer live a lie in any way in my life,
Genuinely living by my lights, truthfully.
I am excited about my choice to do just that.
I love that I strive to live in the
Here and now
And that the only thing that matters
Is the here and now.
I love the clarity
That I needed at that time in my life—
Burning bright
By my own lights!

# Now I Decide

I once really thought I'd like to
see what happens next.
Now I decide.
So I'm not waiting to reply or for your next move.
Now I decide.
What peace and power to choose for myself!
Now I decide.
The only way it will be is if it is so right.
Now I decide.
So instead of waiting on your next move,
I move—by deciding now.

# Do What You've Got to Do

Sometimes it is the last thing
You may have wanted to do,
"But maturity is doing what
You know to do", as Momzi always said.
This too shall pass,
So you just muster up and
Do what you've got to do.
Or do you?
For survival's sake, I sure hope you do.
Only for a season is how long
We were to be, so don't trip—
Just be your very best while you can.
Maturity is doing what you know to do.

# Jams

My sweet jams—
Be it jazz, old school, or even classical—
I just love melodious music and true harmony.
I'm just chillin'! Come join me!
Simple pleasures!
It never has taken much for me.
I just soak it all in
Like a wonderful candlelit bath.
Memories—some take me back.
Love creating new memories too that
Soothe the savage beast within me.
Sweet jams don't just
Have to be slow,
You know!

# Break the Ice

To journey through the unknown—
No, not new, but new to me.
It sometimes takes me a while to literally
Break the ice with myself!
But oh, when I do, it's ever so sweet!
Then I begin to wonder,
*Why have I not done this before?*
*Why did it take me so long to*
*get out of my own way?*
Who cares?
All that matters is that I did
Get out of my own way.
What a blessing to trust and go
With what I don't always know.
What are you waiting for?
Break the ice with yourself!

# Nothing in Vain

Absolutely nothing in my life is in vain,
With every beat, step, and journey
Building on the next.
How wonderfully crafted is the divine design!
I am convinced that my life
Is exactly how it is to be—
The good, the ugly, and
Everything in between.
To accept right now, this
Present moment, is such a gift.
To reflect on the past and know it is to be
Totally changes my outlook
On everything in my life—
Every decision, journey, and obstacle
Was divinely placed there
To teach me who I am becoming
this very moment.
Every step, every stumble, has
Never been in vain.

# Cake and to Eat It Too

Admit it—you really want
Your cake and to eat it too!
Of course you do—if at all possible, right?
Well, you probably already get it,
But not with me.
While you were once my life,
Long dream,
It really has to be right—
Done the right way,
Be in the right timing.
Every aspect must be right, must be
True—no fake;
True—no compromise;
True—no worries;
True—selflessness;
True—just me and you,
At the right times in our lives,
Totally committed to just us two.
Then and only then can you have this cake—
And *you'd better eat* it too!

# You Never Existed

Imagine the world without you—
Like my favorite movie,
*It's a Wonderful Life*,
Everything changed just because
You were not here to
Influence it.
That's the type of reflection
I do regularly.
Ultimately, one never knows just
who and how one impacts.
Just know and believe that your mere existence
Could be the answer to someone's prayers.
I believe that each and every one of us is here
On assignment.
How about you?

# Abundantly Simple

Stripped down to only my necessities,
Learning that less is truly more,
Choosing to purge what I no longer use,
Organizing so that my life just flows
Much more than ever before,
I'm looking to scale down on all
That I have and do.
I've had a new revelation on the
accumulation of things
And am choosing to get rid of excess.
I now abide in my abundantly
Simple life.

# New Reality

Dreams are so weird.
They usually make no sense and pull so many
People together.
I am seeing the power of my
subconscious at work.
Thinking I had not thought
Much about whomever,
I am only to find them starring in my dreams.
Since I really don't remember if I dream,
It's funny when I actually do. I continue to ponder
The healthy thoughts in my life
With an expectation that dreams have become
My desires, which in turn
Have created my new reality.

# Manifestor

I have begun to do work on myself
With an IPod full of personal development
Daily habit journal goals—and so much more—
Only to see them come to fruition.
It's amazing to see how I truly
Am a manifestor,
Creating the life I desire,
Aligning with all that God has for me.
My crystal clear vision
Reminds me that I literally am the architect
Of my life and that I do decide my destiny.

# The Juice

You've got the magnetism that
I just can't explain.
People gravitate to you like you are
A magnet.
You exude peace, joy, and a safety net feeling.
You've got the *juice*.
Just what exactly is the juice?
The *juice* is
Confidence,
Swagger,
Passion,
Love,
Compassion,
And ambition—
Just to name a few.
Having learned to love yourself,
Literally and figuratively,
Like no other—
Baby, you've got the *juice*!

# Choice

Life is all about choices!
To not choose is also a choice.

Today I choose that *smile* equals *gratitude*.
Today I choose to view my glass as
Half full, no matter what.

When I deliberately create,
I live heaven on earth.

Maturity is doing what I know
To do—literally.
Life is what I make of it—
I've chosen.

# My True Love

Grounded is how I feel when I
Just think of you,
Let alone when I am with you.
Joy unspeakable is what you
Give me just by me being in your presence.
Sweetest love I've ever experienced,
You are loyal, committed, and oh so real.
I am so blessed to be given the
ultimate that we all long for—
Unconditional love, day in and day out.
You are so easy to love.
There's never a dull moment,
My true love, my honeypot, my babe!

# Act 3

New book, chapter 1 as we speak.
Then it's act 3—the final act
to an explosive sequel
That is flowing and focused like never before.
How exciting it is to know I am
A few seconds away from an explosion.
Stay steady, girly!
You are soaring like the eagle you always
Knew you were—
Majestic, regal, and proud.
Continue on with your spirit of excellence—
Rule, reign.
Have your being
Be your *best* you!

# True Me

Pure thoughts remain focused,
Saluting the divinity in everyone
No matter what.
I allow my energy to be what I choose it to be
In the midst of chaos,
Stopping and taking seven deep breaths,
Totally relaxing and empowering
at the same time.
I am tapped into *greatness*,
The invisible me,
Reminded that what I give,
I get back—
True reflection,
True me.

# Ciao, Baby!

It's your day—celebrate the day
you entered this universe.
What a gift—
Just being you,
Finding your flow and purpose,
Authentically *doing you*,
Never being afraid of hard work,
Putting your nose to the grind,
And doing it.
I celebrate you.
This is your month.
This is your day.
Ciao, baby!

# Did You Know?

You are oh so beautiful, warm, and charming.
Just being around you is like a drug.
You exude love, confidence, joy, and genuineness.
Many wonder, "Who is she?
Where is the she from?"
So intrigued, many try to get
To know you, only to find
How down-home, warm, caring,
and friendly you are.
Some are shocked because they
Really don't know what to expect,
Having met others who look like you
But don't exude confidence like you do.
It's like a crapshoot to them—
They never know what they will get!

# Holy 'Nother Level

How many do we have?
Everyone's number varies.
Just know that to be who we are,
It's these times that shape us.
You remember every second, all the details,
No matter how long ago
Event(s) happened. Our view on
Life changes is tweaked,
Even if just by a fraction.
It's amazing how that time helps
Take us,
If we allow, to
A holy 'nother level.

# Believe

*Believe* is an *action* word
In the greatest sense of the word.
Everything is in alignment
When belief is as solid as a rock.
*Believe* expects nothing but the best. Also,
It expects what it is supposed to have—
All *God* has for the believer.
No matter what the believer sees,
Belief never expects to
See anything other than what it believes,
What its faith has already put out there.

# Resolve

When do you know that you have
Really resolved to do it?
*Really* do it?
Deep down you believe it;
No matter what you see,
What makes this time's
Commitment different
from the others?
Where does the shift lie?
How do you know you've hit the core?
When do you decide to decide?
When do you draw the line?
Resolve.

# No Longer Exist

When I truly decide to *live* and
No longer *exist*,
I stop *burning daylight* to the max.
I begin to deliberately execute
As I already know I should do.
I pinch myself, to remind me
That the only time that matters
Is *now*—the gift it is
Is the *present*!
It's showtime!
Living second by second,
Minute by minute,
Hour by hour,
Day by day,
And achievement by achievement.

# Sleeping Genius

The more I write, the more I get
To know this awesome lady!
She is intriguing to know.
She is the invisible me,
The greater one inside of me.
Having her reveal herself to me and stay is such
A blessing in my life.
I soar; I fly and acknowledge
All God has for me.
I literally blossom into someone I
Never really got to know
As I have during my life lately.
She's inspirational and classy.
She's me—
My sleeping genius!

# Going for Broke

Taking my foot literally off
The breaks,
Going, as we say, "For broke,"
Which means to take the lid
Off of any endeavor.
Excited to go for broke each
And every day,
I've got nothing to lose and
A full life to live!

# Turbulence

Smooth sailing—there's no such thing.
And if for only a minute
I am reminded that a bump in the
road is not a flat tire—
Just a jar, just a tug—
Everything has meaning, even
When I have no idea what
It means, you know?
Seeking Him first gives me peace,
Relying on His tug, His nudge—
Relying on staying tuned in—
Is worth all the occasional
Turbulence I ever get!

# Act As If

Act *as if*—fake it 'til you make it.
Since I am already living my best life,
I will continue to act as if I have
found my purpose in life.
Since I grow each and every day,
I will continue to act as if
I have unlocked the keys to
Every door I am to open.
Since I want for nothing,
I act as if.
Since I live without concern or worry, I act as if.
I keep my eye on the prize. That's all I see.
I continue to do what I am to do
As God elevates me to no longer have to
Fake it to make it!

# Rebound

Doubt, worry, fear—all of these
Take me off of my game.
I refuse!
I rebound—minute by minute,
Second by second,
And action by action.
This is a new beginning of
Sowing the right seed(s),
No matter what I see.
I have pure thoughts, optimistic thoughts.
I meditate on good,
Expecting good.
Rebounding is all good!

# All-Wheel Drive

What a different feeling it is,
Driving when all tires hug
The road versus just the traditional two wheels.
I am riding the rest of my life on all fours.
I choose to hug the ground and roll.
I choose smooth sailing, with
the pedal to the metal
Allowing me to literally soar like never before!

# Never Miss a Beat

Am I the only one who finds it interesting that
When I finally reconnect with old buddies,
The response or lack of response varies?
Only with a select few is reunion
As though we never lost touch,
We never missed a beat.
So what is it that makes some shy away
When others are open to catch up?
I'll never know.
I just know how I love it when I feel
That we never missed a beat!

# A Rare Commodity

I once lived a life thinking,
"I don't need anybody—I've got this!"
Only to find that none of us
Makes it in life alone.
True friendship—a rare commodity—
Is oh so valuable, I've learned.
No, I am not an island.
One of life's sweetest spices
Is true friendship—
Being there,
Knowing you can count on each other,
Just flowing and being free to
reach out and touch,
And to love from afar and embrace
Literally!
There's nothing like a true friend,
Indeed.

# No

How did you see or view me?
Oh, just another one?
Really? Is that all you've got?
Yep?
Okay, well, excited to get
My perspective back in order,
How do I see or view you?
You're not what I really
Want as a close companion.
I am so excited to regroup
And reveal how things really are *now*!
No, you are no longer that special to me.
I, all of a sudden, feel it is too late!
Let me take just enough time to
Confirm and flow with *no*!

# Best I Can Be

So what's it like just being yourself,
Only to find that you resonate
and minister to so many?
Wonderful!
It's so wonderful to embrace who
God made when He made me.
I'm so thankful to be dropped
off in this earth suit,
Lovin' life like never before
And growing second by second,
Only to show up as the
Greater me,
The invisible me,
In alignment.
I am the best I can be, because
I'm in alignment with the
*greater* me!

# Music, Singing, and Dancing

Music is the heartbeat to my life—
Is and always has been—
So from now on, I will never live
Another day without
Listening to some music.
Dancing is my heartbeat—
Is and always has been.
As I embrace savoring every
Single moment, I continue
To live each day as my last.
My flow is music-singing-dancing.
Think of those three, and
Think of me!

# My Next Fifty

Just like she said to me today—
I'm so excited to live my
Second half,
My second stage,
My act 2,
The second performance
Of my life.
I will live it much as I lived the first fifty—
But truly *not* settling as I did during
Much of the first fifty.
I am not the same person anymore, but I
Love who I am continually.
I am growing to be better
Minute by minute
And day by day.
Better yet—I love who I already am.
I love my *greatness*!

# I Do

Life is not but a measurement
Of time.
I no longer exist—I live.
I savor every single moment.
I do what I know to do.
I get stronger, wiser, and fitter.
I continue to be a better me in every aspect.
I soar like the eagle.
I swim like the dolphin.
I chase like the cougar.
All of that is embedded in me.
I love my quality time.
I love just writing and expressing myself as
I do.

# True Blue

Authentic, original, unforgettable,
Gracious, regal, and unbelievable.
How did He do it?
Creating so originally,
Embracing every single aspect—
He has true acceptance,
True embrace,
And true love
Exploding with the *juice* of life!
The juice splatters on all who are close by,
Spills on all who dare to get drenched
With the most sincere, authentic embrace—
True blue is *you*!

# Eyes Wide Open

I'm just not throwing in the towel.
I really want to see if I can make it work.
I love so much already
And feel I can receive and give back.
I'm staying open right now,
Willing to not jump to any conclusions.
My eyes are wide open!
I'm willing to love unconditionally,
Willing to see if it can be really true.
You have qualities I already love:
Faithfulness,
Dedication,
Love,
Adoration of me,
Demonstration of appreciation,
Attentiveness,
Keeping lifted to *God*, and
Enjoying the here and now.

# My Promise to You

I promised you I would know when to let go.
The decision was not easy; I need
you to know that it's been
Seventeen years almost that
we've been together—
Through thick and thin and any kind of weather.
You exceeded my expectations
in each and every way,
Making my last seventeen years the best life
I've ever had.
As selfish as it sounds, I wanted
to keep you here forever.
To genuinely love you was to
release you and let go—
No more pain, discomfort, or
threat of further attack.
You have lived a full, good, and loved-filled life.
Many would love the same,
But I can only speak regarding you when I say
God did not duplicate you in any way whatsoever.
I love you Tater Tot, my Honeypot, my Babe,
My sixteen-year-old Lhasa Apso, Latte.

# Awesome Gift of You!

Best friend and mom—what a blessing!
I knew this day would never be easy.
I just wanted to be there every second
As you have been in my life,
Day in and day out,
Present in every moment, there.
I believe all moms are special.
You broke the mold, though.
My goal was to always just be there
Through the thick and thin, as
you always were with us.
I enjoyed knowing you knew I
would not only be there
But be who you could count on.
Of all your worldly accomplishments,
We (O and I) were your proudest!
I miss you horribly—the void is real.
While I am reminded that I carry you in my heart,
In my pocket, in my life, and in my face,
You are right here with me every step of the way.
Who ever knew that one's own mom would
Turn out to be one's *best* friend ever?
Thanks for giving me your awesome gift of you!

# Cabo Day

My favorite vacation destination
is Cabo San Lucas.
The beach calls me as though
I was conceived there.
The ocean soothes my soul.
While others do excursions,
I chill on the beach with a good book, nail polish,
Or nothing, just taking it all in.
Once I am home, to recreate my Zen
I have a Cabo Day.
I put on my bikini under my T-shirt.
I may put on a sarong.
I go on my patio,
My oasis,
And just chillax—
My home-grown Cabo Day.

Savoi Rags is a fun-loving individual who embraces all of who she is and continues to evolve to be. Always looking to grow as a person, the author is reflective; a self-proclaimed 'after-thoughter' mostly to self-evaluate and/or simply learn from yet another life lesson. The author resides in Denver, Colorado.

Printed in the United States
By Bookmasters